Irish Butterflies and Insects

Dr Eugenie Regan
and Chris Shields

First published in 2009 by
Appletree Press Ltd
The Old Potato Station
14 Howard Street South
Belfast BT7 1AP

Tel: +44 (028) 90 24 30 74
Fax: +44 (028) 90 24 67 56
Email: reception@appletree.ie
Web: www.appletree.ie

Copyright © Appletree Press, 2009
Text by Dr Eugenie Regan
Illustrations © Chris Shields

Irish Butterflies and Insects

ISBN-13: 978 1 84758 121 1

Desk and Marketing Editor: Jean Brown
Copy-editor: Jim Black
Designer: Stuart Wilkinson
Production Manager: Paul McAvoy

9 8 7 6 5 4 3 2 1

AP3603

Contents

Contents

Introduction

This pocket guide is an introduction to the fascinating, hidden world of Irish insects. Ireland's insects are the most abundant and diverse animals in Ireland yet they are an overlooked and neglected part of Ireland's fauna.

With over 12,000 known species of insects in Ireland, this book has been divided into the major groups with general descriptions of those groups so that most insects encountered could be categorised by a beginner. Descriptions of the more commonly encountered species are given along with illustrations.

What is an insect? Insects come in many shapes and forms, from beetles to bugs and from earwigs to butterflies. A standard definition is that an insect has six legs and the adult body is divided into three distinct parts: the head, the thorax, and the abdomen. Insects usually have two pairs of wings and in the case of beetles the first set have been modified into wing cases.

Insects are the most diverse group of animals on the Earth. They are grouped together by scientists in the Class Insecta of which there are 13 orders in Ireland, including the Order Coleoptera (beetles), Order Diptera (flies), and the Order Lepidoptera (butterflies and moths).

Butterflies and moths
There are over 1,400 species of butterflies and moths in Ireland. They are among the most beautiful, charismatic, and fragile of all Irish insects.

There are just over 30 species of butterfly in Ireland, so the moths are a lot more specious and difficult to identify. But butterflies are relatively easily identified. Eleven species are illustrated here and these should help you begin to recognise the butterflies in your garden and local area.

Butterflies and moths go through four life stages: egg, larva (caterpillar), chrysalis and adult (see the illustration on the opposite page).

The butterfly eggs are usually laid on plants and are fixed to the leaf with special glue that hardens rapidly. Butterfly larvae, or caterpillars, consume plant leaves and spend practically all of their time in search of or eating food. When the caterpillar is fully grown, hormones are produced. At this point the caterpillar stops feeding and starts searching for a suitable pupation site, often the underside of a leaf. The caterpillar anchors itself to the leaf and moults for the last time. It transforms into an adult butterfly through metamorphosis.

The adult has four membranous wings with minute overlapping scales, usually brightly coloured.

How to find Irish insects
Insects are found practically everywhere! Moths are easily found at an outside light in the evening, beetles can be found running around in the garden or under stones and logs, ants exploring a nearby field, wasps looking for some sugar at a picnic, and bees for nectar at a flower in the garden.

While insects are easy to observe, some basic equipment can be very useful when learning about insects in more detail. A butterfly net is essential when learning the different butterfly species. It is also handy for catching dragonflies and damselflies, bees and wasps, hoverflies, and other larger flying insects. A simple jam jar can be placed in a hole flush with the ground and this can be very effective at catching ground

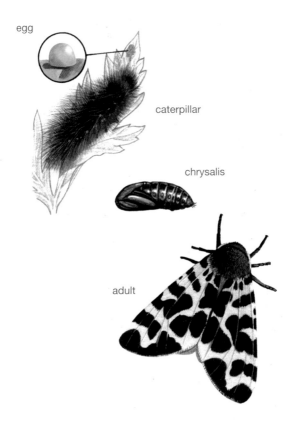

egg

caterpillar

chrysalis

adult

The life cycle of the garden tiger moth

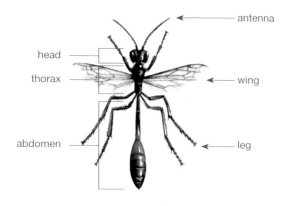

antenna

head

thorax

wing

abdomen

leg

Anatomy of an insect

beetles, ants, and other insects. A hand lens is needed for identifying most of the larger insects while a microscope is essential for looking at smaller animals (most insects are less than 5mm long!). Binoculars are also useful for spotting butterflies and dragonflies.

Further reading
Irish insects are a poorly studied group in general. However, there are a few guides that will aid anybody interested in learning more about this group. If you're interested in what's lurking in the corners of your house *Irish Indoor Insects: A Popular Guide* by James P. O'Connor and Patrick Ashe is an essential guide. Michael Chinery's *Insects of Britain and Western Europe* has an excellent key to the insect families with illustrations of a good number of species, while Richard Lewington's *Guide to Garden Wildlife* is another beautifully illustrated book that is an excellent introduction to these fascinating animals. With over 12,000 species, specialist identification books are needed to identify most insects to species level. Peter C. Barnard's *Identifying British Insects and Arachnids* is a good place to find the appropriate information.

The reader should note that illustrations are not to scale and that the illustrations will simply help identify what group an animal belongs to rather than identify a particular species.

Large White
Pieris brassicae

Large White

The Large White is considered a pest by many Irish gardeners as the caterpillars love to munch on garden vegetables. For this reason it is also called the 'Cabbage Butterfly' or 'Cabbage White'.

Where to see:

This butterfly is very mobile and can be seen in most parts of Ireland. Most adults are seen close to breeding areas, such as gardens and crop fields.

Identification:

The Large White is our largest butterfly and the strongest flyer. Adults have large white wings with broad black tips on the forewings. Males can be distinguished from females as they lack the two black spots and black streak on each forewing seen in the illustration opposite.

What they eat:

The adults drink nectar from flowers while the caterpillars feed on wild or cultivated species of the cabbage family with a strong preference for cultivated varieties such as cabbage and Brussel sprouts.

When to see:

Jan	Feb	Mar	Apr	May	Jun	Jul	Aug	Sep	Oct	Nov	Dec
				■	■		■				

male

female

Orange Tip
Anthocharis cardamines

Orange Tip

The Orange Tip along with the Primrose (*Primula vulgaris*) and Cuckoo (*Cuculus canorus*), is a true herald of spring. It is one of the few butterfly species that are on the increase in Ireland. The adults live for about 18 days, with one generation per year.

Where to see:

This is a widespread species throughout Ireland and can be easily spotted in hedgerows and gardens.

Identification:

The males have white wings with orange wing tips while the females are white with black wing tips. The male is much more conspicuous and more frequently seen than the female. The female can be confused with the small white. The Orange Tip is the only white butterfly with mottled green underwing markings.

What they eat:

A wide variety of plants of the cabbage family may be used for food, but caterpillars prefer the Cuckoo Flower (*Cardamine pratensis*) and Watercress (*Rorippa nasturtium-aquaticum*).

When to see:

Jan	Feb	Mar	Apr	May	Jun	Jul	Aug	Sep	Oct	Nov	Dec

Common Blue
Polyommatus icarus

Common Blue

The Common Blue is a small, widespread butterfly that has an unusual relationship with ants. The caterpillars secrete a substance that attracts ants. In turn, the ants protect the caterpillars from predators.

Where to see:

It is widespread across the country and is found in a variety of grassy habitats basking in the sun.

Identification:

The males and females are quite distinct. The upperwings of the male are blue while those of the female are brown to deep-violet blue. The underside of the wings make this butterfly easily distinguishable from the other blues due to a series of orange spots at the outer margins which are absent in the other Irish blue butterflies.

What they eat:

Bird's-foot Trefoil (*Lotus corniculatus*) is the main larval foodplant. Other plants used include White Clover (*Trifolium repens*) and Black Medick (*Medicago lupulina*). The adults feed on nectar from flat-headed flowers.

When to see:

Jan	Feb	Mar	Apr	May	Jun	Jul	Aug	Sep	Oct	Nov	Dec

Holly Blue
Celastrina argiolus

Holly Blue

The Holly Blue emerges well before the other blues in early spring. Interestingly this butterfly is double brooded from Dublin southwards and single brooded in the north.

Where to see:

It is found in woodlands, urban parks and gardens where Holly and Ivy are present.

Identification:

There are three blue butterflies in Ireland. The Common Blue has orange spots on its underwing, and the Small Blue (*Cupido minimus*) is a small butterfly that is rare in Ireland and often overlooked. The Holly Blue is easily distinguished from these two by its bright blue wings and lack of the orange spots on the underwing. It is often seen flying around Holly trees.

What they eat:

In the spring the caterpillars feed on Holly (*Ilex aquifolium*) and in the summer they feed on Ivy (*Hedera helix*) as well as other plants. The adults tend to feed on the flowers of Holly and Ivy.

When to see:

Jan	Feb	Mar	Apr	May	Jun	Jul	Aug	Sep	Oct	Nov	Dec

Red Admiral
Vanessa atalanta

Red Admiral

The Red Admiral is one of our migrant species, migrating northwards from the Mediterranean and arriving in Ireland in May. The immigrant females lay eggs and new adults emerge in late summer. Adults try to hibernate in Ireland but they do not survive the Irish winters.

Where to see:

The Red Admiral is widespread in Ireland and can be found feeding on a variety of flowers and basking in the sunshine. It is found in most Irish habitats in urban and rural locations.

Identification:

This is a distinctive butterfly having dark brown/black wings with orange-red bands. The forewing tips are black with white spots. It is also one of our largest butterflies.

What they eat:

The most important larval foodplant is the Common Nettle (*Urtica dioica*). The adults drink nectar from flowers with the Buddleia (*Buddleja davidii*) a favourite.

When to see:

Jan	Feb	Mar	Apr	May	Jun	Jul	Aug	Sep	Oct	Nov	Dec

Painted Lady
Vanessa cardui

Painted Lady

The Painted Lady is another migrant butterfly. The main breeding ground is Southern Europe and North Africa. It migrates to Northern Europe and Ireland and is most commonly seen in late summer. During autumn the Irish population die or return to Africa.

Where to see:

The adults can be seen feeding on a variety of nectar-rich flowers in most habitats.

Identification:

The adults have orange-brown wings with white spots on the forewings. It is a distinctive butterfly and the most similar species is the Red Admiral.

What they eat:

A wide range of larval food plants may be used, in particular Thistles (*Cirsium* spp.) and Nettles (*Urtica* spp.).

When to see:

Jan	Feb	Mar	Apr	May	Jun	Jul	Aug	Sep	Oct	Nov	Dec

Small Tortoiseshell
Aglais urticae

Small Tortoiseshell

The Small Tortoiseshell is amongst the best-known butterflies in Ireland as it regularly frequents gardens and can often be found hibernating in houses. Adults emerge from hibernation in spring to look for mates.

Where to see:

This species is widespread in Ireland and can be seen in almost any habitat.

Identification:

This is a distinctive butterfly. The adults have bright orange and black wings with a row of blue crescents around the wing edges. Underneath they are dark grey and brown.

What they eat:

The caterpillars feed on the Common Nettle (*Urtica dioica*) while the adults drink nectar from flowers with the favourite being Buddleia (*Buddleja davidii*).

When to see:

Jan	Feb	Mar	Apr	May	Jun	Jul	Aug	Sep	Oct	Nov	Dec

Peacock
Inachis io

Peacock

The Peacock is a well-known colourful butterfly that gets its name from the large eyespots on their wings, which resemble those on the tail of the peacock.

Where to see:

It is common and widespread in Ireland being seen in most habitats where there are lots of flowers.

Identification:

This butterfly is distinctive with red wings and eyespots on both the forewings and hindwings. The caterpillars are black with small white spots and black spines along their back and sides.

What they eat:

The adults feed on nectar from flowers such as Thistles (*Cirsium* spp.) and Buddleia (*Buddleja davidii*). They will also feed on over-ripe fruit in late summer. The main food plant of the caterpillar is Nettles (*Urtica dioica*).

When to see:

Jan	Feb	Mar	Apr	May	Jun	Jul	Aug	Sep	Oct	Nov	Dec

Speckled Wood
Pararge aegeria

Speckled Wood

This brown woodland butterfly is rarely seen on flowers as it prefers to eat aphid honeydew rather than nectar.

Where to see:

The Speckled Wood is widespread and common in Ireland and can be seen at hedgerows and in open areas of woodlands.

Identification:

There are a few brown butterflies in Ireland but this is the only one that is dull brown in colour with cream spots. It has a wingspan of approximately 50mm.

What they eat:

The adults feed on aphid honeydew which is a sugary substance that is secreted by aphids as they feed on plant sap. Speckled Wood caterpillars feed on various grasses.

When to see:

Jan	Feb	Mar	Apr	May	Jun	Jul	Aug	Sep	Oct	Nov	Dec

male

female

Meadow Brown
Maniola jurtina

Meadow Brown

This is a common butterfly found almost everywhere in Ireland.

Where to see:

Meadow Browns are widespread and common in Ireland and are found in fields, roadsides and woodland margins.

Identification:

Adults are brown and orange with a black eyespot on the forewing tip. They can be confused with the rarer Gatekeeper (*Pyronia tithonus*) but only have one white spot in the black eyespot whereas the Gatekeeper has two.

What they eat:

The adults feed on nectar from Thistles (*Cirsium* spp.) and Knapweed (*Centaurea* spp.) flowers. The caterpillars feed on a variety of grasses.

When to see:

Jan	Feb	Mar	Apr	May	Jun	Jul	Aug	Sep	Oct	Nov	Dec

Ringlet
Aphantopus hyperantus

Ringlet

The Ringlet is a pretty brown butterfly that is found throughout Ireland.

Where to see:

It is widespread and common in Ireland being found in meadows and hedgerows.

Identification:

The Ringlet is easily identified by its brown colouration and five spots on the underside of the hindwing. The only similar species in Ireland is the Large Heath (*Coenonympha tullia*) which has a much lighter, orange colouration.

What they eat:

The adults feed on nectar. Ringlet caterpillars feed on various grasses, including Cock's-foot (*Dactylis glomerata*) and Meadow Grasses (*Poa* spp.).

When to see:

Jan	Feb	Mar	Apr	May	Jun	Jul	Aug	Sep	Oct	Nov	Dec

Large Yellow Underwing
Noctua pronuba

Large Yellow Underwing

The Large Yellow Underwing (*Noctua pronuba*) is the most common and familiar moths in Ireland. Its caterpillar is one of the most hated garden pests.

Where to see:

This moth is common and widely distributed across Ireland being found in a wide range of habitats.

Identification:

During the day, this species rests near the ground amongst grass. It has dull brown upperwings and when disturbed flashes its bright yellow and black underwings in an effort to surprise an attacker. Consult an expert for definitive species identification.

What they eat:

The caterpillars feed mainly underground on a range of wild and cultivated herbs and grasses which gives rise to their common name 'cutworms' as they cause damage to plants by cutting through the growing stem. The adults feed on liquid nectar.

When to see:

Jan	Feb	Mar	Apr	May	Jun	Jul	Aug	Sep	Oct	Nov	Dec

White Ermine
Spilosoma lubricipeda

White Ermine

The White Ermine moth is widely distributed and commonly encountered in most Irish counties.

Where to see:

It is found in a variety of habitats including hedgerows and urban gardens.

Identification:

The key identification features are the white forewings with small black dots, large hairy thorax and yellow abdomen with black dorsal bars. There is considerable variation in the degree of black speckling.

What they eat:

The caterpillars feed on a variety of herbaceous plants while the adults feed on liquid nectar.

When to see:

Jan	Feb	Mar	Apr	May	Jun	Jul	Aug	Sep	Oct	Nov	Dec

Elephant Hawk-moth
Deilephila elpenor

Elephant Hawk-moth

The Elephant Hawk-moth is a handsome moth that is found throughout Ireland. The common name is derived from the caterpillar's apparent resemblance to an elephant's trunk.

Where to see:

This moth is widespread in Ireland and can be found in a variety of habitats including gardens, waste ground, and woodland clearings.

Identification:

The adults are attractively coloured pink and green and a streamlined appearance. The key identification features for this moth is the size (62mm-72mm), pink stripe on forewings, and pink hindwings. It can be confused with the Small Elephant Hawk-moth, *Deilephila porccellus*.

What they eat:

The preferred food plants of the caterpillar are Willowherb (*Epilobium* spp.) and Bedstraw (*Galium* spp.). The adults feed on liquid nectar.

When to see:

Jan	Feb	Mar	Apr	May	Jun	Jul	Aug	Sep	Oct	Nov	Dec

Magpie Moth
Abraxas grossulariata

Magpie Moth

This is a distinctive moth which uses its bold colours to alert predators that it is distasteful. Even spiders will not eat this moth and interestingly, it appears to have immunity to spider venom.

Where to see:

It is frequently seen in gardens, and also in woodlands, hedgerows and coastal habitats.

Identification:

This is a highly variable species with many different forms, however it is unlikely to be confused with any other species. It has a distinctive speckled black and white colouration and a wingspan of 42-48mm.

What they eat:

The caterpillars feed on a variety of plants and shrubs including Blackthorn (*Prunus spinosa*), Hawthorn (*Crataegus monogyna*), and Hazel (*Corylus avellana*). The adults feed on liquid nectar.

When to see:

Jan	Feb	Mar	Apr	May	Jun	Jul	Aug	Sep	Oct	Nov	Dec

Silver Y
Autographa gamma

Silver Y

The Silver Y is mainly a migrant moth with adults arriving in early summer. There are usually two broods a year. Adults are killed by frost in the autumn, but some may overwinter.

Where to see:

It is widespread and common across Ireland. It is active by day as well as dusk and can be found in a variety of habitats from woodland to coastal grassland.

Identification:

The Silver Y has pale brown wings with a distinctive silvery white Y-shaped marking on each forewing.

What they eat:

The adults feed on nectar while the caterpillars feed on a variety of low-growing plants.

When to see:

Jan	Feb	Mar	Apr	May	Jun	Jul	Aug	Sep	Oct	Nov	Dec

Garden Tiger
Arctia caja

Garden Tiger

The Garden Tiger is a stout, hairy moth whose bright colours warn predators that it tastes unpleasant.

Where to see:

This moth is widespread and common in Ireland. The adults are rarely encountered during the day and are more likely to be seen at night when they are attracted to lights.

Identification:

The adults have brown and white markings on the forewings and red hindwings with dark blue spots. It is difficult to confuse with any other species. The caterpillars are commonly referred to as 'woolly bears' as they are brown and black and exceedingly hairy. The hairs are 'irritant' and protect it from predators – don't pick one up!

What they eat:

The caterpillars feed on a variety of wild and garden plants. The adults drink nectar from flowers.

When to see:

Jan	Feb	Mar	Apr	May	Jun	Jul	Aug	Sep	Oct	Nov	Dec
					■	■	■				

Large Red Damselfly
Pyrrhosoma nymphula

Large Red Damselfly

The Large Red Damselfly is often the first damselfly on the wing in late April or May. It is one of the most common damselflies in Ireland. Dragonflies and damselflies are fascinating insects that spend the first part of their lives underwater as nymphs. The nymphs eventually climb out of the water up a plant stem to emerge from their split skins as dragonflies or damselflies.

Where to see:

The Large Red Damselfly can be seen resting on vegetation near water.

Identification:

This is the only species of red damselfly in Ireland making it easily recognisable.

What they eat:

Both adults and nymphs are predators feeding on smaller insects.

When to see:

Jan	Feb	Mar	Apr	May	Jun	Jul	Aug	Sep	Oct	Nov	Dec
				■	■	■	■				

Common Blue Damselfly
Enallagma cyathigerum

Common Blue Damselfly

The small, brightly coloured Common Blue Damselfly is probably the most widespread member of the dragonfly and damselfly family in Ireland.

Where to see:

It can be seen at lake edges amongst emergent vegetation.

Identification:

This species is the 'bluest' of the blue damselflies and is similar to the Azure Damselfly (*Coenagrion puella*), the Variable Damselfly (*Coenagrion pulchellum*), and the Irish Damselfly (*Coenagrion lunulatum*). One of the key identification features is the black club-shaped mark on the second abdominal segment as seen in the illustration opposite.

What they eat:

Both adults and nymphs are predators and feed on smaller insects.

When to see:

Jan	Feb	Mar	Apr	May	Jun	Jul	Aug	Sep	Oct	Nov	Dec

Brown Hawker
Aeshna grandis

Brown Hawker

The Brown Hawker is one of the largest species of dragonfly in Ireland with adults measuring over 70mm in length. It is highly territorial and will defend its stretch of water against any visitors.

Where to see:

This species is locally common and widespread in Ireland and is found in sheltered lowland lakes and fens. Adults can wander some distances from their breeding habitats.

Identification:

Both sexes are brown with tinted amber wings. There are two pale yellow stripes on the side of the thorax and males have a waisted abdomen with blue spots on the side.

What they eat:

Both adults and nymphs are predators and feed on smaller insects.

When to see:

Jan	Feb	Mar	Apr	May	Jun	Jul	Aug	Sep	Oct	Nov	Dec
					▓	▓	▓	▓			

Ground Beetle
Pterostichus madidus

Ground Beetle

Ground beetles or carabids are a large beetle family with 211 species in Ireland. A specialist book and microscope is needed to identify them properly. The species illustrated here, *Pterostichus madidus*, is one of the most common Irish species.

Where to see:

Ground beetles are most often encountered sheltering under stones in the garden.

Identification:

Pterostichus madidus is a large shiny black ground beetle measuring 15-20mm in length. A hand lens or microscope and specialist key are needed to accurately identify ground beetles.

What they eat:

Most carabids are carnivorous and actively hunt for any invertebrate prey they can overpower.

When to see:

Jan	Feb	Mar	Apr	May	Jun	Jul	Aug	Sep	Oct	Nov	Dec

Green Tiger Beetle
Cicindela campestris

Green Tiger Beetle

Tiger beetles are closely related to ground beetles. They are long-legged, fast hunters that are characterised by their metallic and iridescent colours.

Where to see:

Tiger beetles are active during sunny days and can be seen in sandy habitats such as sand dunes and shores of rivers and streams. They can be seen basking in the sun and running or flying away quickly when approached.

Identification:

There is only one species of tiger beetle in Ireland, the Green Tiger Beetle (*Cicindela campestris*). It is a bright green beetle and could only be confused with ground beetles. This beetle is distinguished by its bright green colour, large, bulbous, wide-set eyes, and fast movement.

What they eat:

Tiger beetles are predators and both the adults and larvae feed on a wide variety of other insects.

When to see:

Jan	Feb	Mar	Apr	May	Jun	Jul	Aug	Sep	Oct	Nov	Dec

Devil's Coach Horse
Ocypus olens

Devil's Coach Horse

The Devil's Coach Horse is a common and widespread beetle belonging to the large family of rove beetles. There are about 640 species in the rove beetle family and many are difficult to identify. The Devil's Coach Horse is well known for its habit of raising its long abdomen and opening its jaws when threatened. This beetle has been associated with the devil since the Middle Ages, hence its common name.

Where to see:

This black beetle usually shelters during the day under stones, logs or leaf litter.

Identification:

It is one of the largest Irish beetles with a length of about 25-28mm. These beetles are difficult to identify and easily confused with other species.

What they eat:

It is a predator feeding on invertebrates including woodlice and worms. It mainly hunts by night. The larvae are also carnivorous with similar eating habits.

When to see:

Jan	Feb	Mar	Apr	May	Jun	Jul	Aug	Sep	Oct	Nov	Dec

Soldier Beetle
Rhagonycha fulva

Soldier Beetle

Rhagonycha fulva is the most common of the 27 species of soldier beetle found in Ireland. It is a familiar sight in summer, especially on the flower heads of umbellifers such as Hogweed (*Heracleum sphondylium*).

Where to see:

Soldier beetles are seen on flower heads in the summer feeding, basking in the sun and mating. They are found in a variety of habitats throughout Ireland.

Identification:

Many members of the soldier beetle family are brightly coloured and they can be difficult to identify. *Rhagonycha fulva* is orange and the tips of the wing-cases are black. It is typically 7-10mm in length.

What they eat:

Soldier beetles feed on other small insects that feed on flowers.

When to see:

Jan	Feb	Mar	Apr	May	Jun	Jul	Aug	Sep	Oct	Nov	Dec

Seven-spot Ladybird
Coccinella septempunctata

Seven-spot Ladybird

Ladybird beetles are probably the most well known of all insects. In Ireland there are 18 different species of ladybird. The ladybird's bright colours are a warning to predators of its foul taste. Ladybirds are beneficial garden insects as both adults and larvae feed on many different garden pests including aphids, greenflies, whiteflies, mealybugs and other scale insects.

Where to see:

The Seven-spot Ladybird is the commonest ladybird across Ireland and can be seen in most habitats except the uplands.

Identification:

This beetle is easily recognised by the red wing cases with seven black spots. The larvae are black and spiky with yellow spots and are occasionally called 'insect alligators'.

What they eat:

The adults and larvae feed on aphids and because of this are useful for pest control on crops.

When to see:

Jan	Feb	Mar	Apr	May	Jun	Jul	Aug	Sep	Oct	Nov	Dec

Vine Weevil
Otiorhynchus sulcatus

Vine Weevil

The Vine Weevil has become a serious pest in recent years attacking many garden plants including Fuchsia (*Fuchsia magellanica*). Although the adult weevil does not do much damage, it is the larval stage that is the real threat.

Where to see:

It is common in gardens throughout Ireland where it eats U-shaped pieces from the edge of leaves of shrubs, especially Rhododendron (*Rhododendron ponticum*), earning the nickname of 'ticket collector'.

Identification:

The adults are dark brown round-backed beetles. The larva is a crescent-shaped white maggot which lives below the soil surface.

What they eat:

The adults feed on the leaves of evergreen trees and shrubs while the larvae feed on the roots.

When to see:

Jan	Feb	Mar	Apr	May	Jun	Jul	Aug	Sep	Oct	Nov	Dec

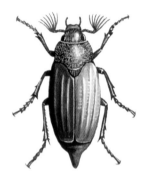

Cockchafer
Melolontha melolontha

Cockchafer

The Cockchafer is a night flier that often comes crashing into lighted windows on warm evenings in early summer. They are sometimes called the 'Maybug' because of the month they normally appear. They have a three-year life cycle most of which is spent as a larvae in the soil. Adults only live for five to seven weeks.

Where to see:

This beetle is found throughout Ireland and can be seen flying at dusk from May to July.

Identification:

These are large beetles (25-35mm long) which make a buzzing noise in flight. Cockchafer larvae are a creamy-white colour with a brown head and range from 2-25mm in length as they grow in size.

What they eat:

The larvae eat plant roots and can do damage to cereal crops and grasses. The adults chew flowers and leaves.

When to see:

Jan	Feb	Mar	Apr	May	Jun	Jul	Aug	Sep	Oct	Nov	Dec

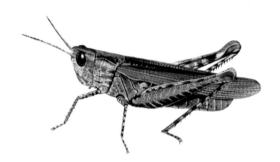

Common Field Grasshopper
Chorthippus brunneus

Common Field Grasshopper

The songs of these attractive, often large insects are closely associated with warm, sunny days and have become associated with memories of good summers. The range of sounds they produce are unique to each different species. The Common Field Grasshopper is the most frequently found grasshopper in urban gardens.

Where to see:

It is widespread in eastern and southern Ireland and confined to the coast in other parts of the country. It is a warmth-loving grasshopper that is most abundant in short, dry grassland.

Identification:

The Common Field Grasshopper, (*Chorthippus brunneus*), is usually pale brown in colour, though it can be partly or entirely green. A specialist key and hand lens or microscope are required for certain identification.

What they eat:

Grasshoppers mostly eat grass.

When to see:

Jan	Feb	Mar	Apr	May	Jun	Jul	Aug	Sep	Oct	Nov	Dec

Common Earwig
Forficula auricularia

Common Earwig

We have three species of earwig in Ireland, with *Forficula auricularia* being the most common. Despite its name and threatening appearance, the Common Earwig is a harmless and interesting insect. The females lay eggs under stones and in crevices and will guard her young until they have grown large enough to fend for themselves.

Where to see:

They are nocturnal animals and can be found sheltering in cracks and crevices during the day.

Identification:

Earwigs are distinctive animals easily recognised by the characteristic pincers at the end of their body. The Common Earwig is shiny and dark chestnut-brown in colour. It measures around 10-15mm in length. The two other Irish species are smaller and rarely encountered.

What they eat:

Earwigs are omnivorous, eating flowers and small insects, amongst other things.

When to see:

Jan	Feb	Mar	Apr	May	Jun	Jul	Aug	Sep	Oct	Nov	Dec

Dronefly
Eristalis tenax

Dronefly

The dronefly is a member of the hoverfly family. Hoverflies can closely resemble bees or wasps but in fact they are true flies and can't sting. They mimic bees and wasps so that they are avoided by predators. There are 180 different hoverfly species in Ireland.

Where to see:

As their name suggests they are often seen hovering at flowers or guarding their territory. They are found in a range of habitats throughout Ireland.

Identification:

Hoverflies are very good mimics and with over 180 species in Ireland, they can be difficult to identify. In many cases, a microscope and specialist key is needed. The species shown in the illustration, the Dronefly, *Eristalis tenax*, closely resembles a Honeybee.

What they eat:

Hoverfly adults drink nectar and also eat pollen and honeydew. The larvae are more specialised with different species eating different things.

When to see:

Jan	Feb	Mar	Apr	May	Jun	Jul	Aug	Sep	Oct	Nov	Dec

Mosquito
Culicidae

Mosquito

There are 17 species of mosquito in Ireland. The females of most mosquito species suck blood from other animals, which has made them one of the most deadly disease vector known. The female produces the characteristic whining sound by vibrating thin horny membranes on the thorax.

Where to see:

Their breeding habitat is water, including ditches, ponds, and water butts in the garden.

Identification:

Mosquitoes can easily be confused with other non-biting insects. The main features to look out for are the long pointed proboscis (the feeding mouthpart) and the wings which are folded and flat when at rest.

What they eat:

Both male and female mosquitoes are nectar feeders, but the females of many species are also capable of drinking blood. Females do not require blood for their own survival and the blood protein is actually used to develop eggs.

When to see:

Jan	Feb	Mar	Apr	May	Jun	Jul	Aug	Sep	Oct	Nov	Dec

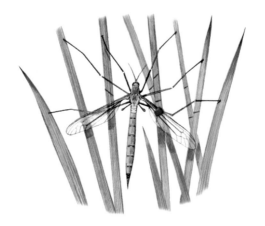

Common Cranefly
Tipula paludosa

Common Cranefly

This very common long-legged fly is also known as the 'Daddy Long Legs'. They have very fragile legs which can easily break off when handling. *Tipula paludosa* is also called the 'September Cranefly' as its numbers peak in this month.

Where to see:

Craneflies are found throughout Ireland and are often attracted to lights at night. They are normally found in fields with short grass. In September the females can be seen bobbing up and down in grassland as they lay their eggs.

Identification:

Tipula paludosa is about 25mm long and has plain grey wings and a pale brown body.

What they eat:

Adult flies rarely feed. The larvae are the infamous root-eating 'Leatherjackets' and can seriously damage crops.

When to see:

Jan	Feb	Mar	Apr	May	Jun	Jul	Aug	Sep	Oct	Nov	Dec

Blue Bottle Fly
Calliphora vomitoria

Blue Bottle Fly

The Blue Bottle is a well-known fly in Ireland as it comes into houses looking for uncovered meat in which to lay its eggs.

Where to see:

This fly is common and widespread in Ireland.

Identification:

It is 10-14mm long with a bright metallic blue abdomen. Its legs and body are covered in black bristle-like hairs. The eyes are red and the wings are clear.

What they eat:

Blue Bottles eat the decaying bodies of dead animals and faeces making them essential organisms in the breakdown of waste. As they use dead material as their main food source and as a place to lay their eggs, they are key to the ecological lifecycle by 'recycling' nutrients in the waste.

When to see:

Jan	Feb	Mar	Apr	May	Jun	Jul	Aug	Sep	Oct	Nov	Dec

queen

worker

Honeybee
Apis mellifera

Honeybee

Honeybees are bees that are primarily distinguished by their production and storage of honey and the production of perennial, colonial nests out of wax. *Apis mellifera* has been domesticated by humans since the time of the building of the Egyptian pyramids. They live in large colonies in bee hives with a queen, hundreds of female workers, and some male drones. They make honey from pollen and nectar gathered from flowers.

Where to see:

Honeybees can be seen anywhere with plenty of flowers, including urban gardens, parks, and orchards.

Identification:

There are over 100 bee species in Ireland yet there is only one species of honeybee. They can be confused with solitary bees and with some hoverflies. Bees can be distinguished from hoverflies as they have two pairs of wings. Differentiating between bee species is more complex and specialist keys are needed.

What they eat:

Honeybees collect nectar and pollen from nearby flowers to bring back to the hive for immediate consumption as well as storage as honey.

When to see:

Jan	Feb	Mar	Apr	May	Jun	Jul	Aug	Sep	Oct	Nov	Dec

Common Carder Bumblebee
Bombus pascuorum

Common Carder Bumblebee

There are 19 species of bumblebee in Ireland. Bumblebees are social insects that live in colonies consisting of a queen, female workers and males. The workers and males look similar to the queen but are smaller. Bumblebees are most often seen on sunny summer days visiting flowers in the garden. They are important pollinators of crops and wild flowers.

Where to see:

The Common Carder Bumblebee, *Bombus pascuorum*, is a widely found in Ireland and can be seen in a range of habitats, including urban gardens and parks.

Identification:

This is a gingery-brown bee and is the 'brownest' of our bumblebees.

What they eat:

Bumblebees feed on nectar and pollen. This species is a long-tongued bee which prefers flowers with a long tube such as red and white clover. The larvae are fed directly by the workers on a combination of nectar and pollen.

When to see:

Jan	Feb	Mar	Apr	May	Jun	Jul	Aug	Sep	Oct	Nov	Dec

Common Wasp
Vespula vulgaris

Common Wasp

The Common Wasp, *Vespula vulgaris*, is a 'typical' black and yellow wasp. It is a social wasp which forms colonies above ground in enclosed spaces such as cavity walls, attics, or hollow trees. Sometimes the papery nests are built underground in an existing cavity such as a mouse nest.

Where to see:

This wasp is common and widespread in Ireland and is usually seen in numbers in gardens from mid-summer and into the autumn when it is attracted to picnics or rotting fallen fruits.

Identification:

A distinctive insect, the common wasp is 17-20mm long and has alternating black and yellow stripes on its abdomen. It can be confused with the German Wasp, *Vespula germanica*, which is smaller and has three tiny black dots on its face.

What they eat:

It is mainly predatory on other insects but also feeds on bruised fruit and nectar. The adults collect insects to feed its larvae.

When to see:

Jan	Feb	Mar	Apr	May	Jun	Jul	Aug	Sep	Oct	Nov	Dec

Sand Digger Wasp
Ammophila sabulosa

Sand Digger Wasp

The Sand Digger Wasp is a parasitoid wasp. These are a group of wasps which lay their eggs on or in other insects. The egg hatches and the parasitoid larva eats the host alive before emerging as an adult. There are approximately 3,000 species of parasitoid wasps in Ireland many of which are very small. They are a poorly known group and difficult to identify.

Where to see:

Adults are visible as adults from late spring to early autumn feeding at flowers. Parasitoid wasps are extremely common in all habitats in Ireland but are easily overlooked.

Identification:

The parasitoid wasp in the illustration is commonly called the Sand Digger Wasp, *Ammophila sabulosa*, and is widely seen in gardens at flowers. It is about 20mm long with an orange and black waisted abdomen.

What they eat:

The larvae are carnivorous feeding on their host while the adults are generally pollen feeders.

When to see:

Jan	Feb	Mar	Apr	May	Jun	Jul	Aug	Sep	Oct	Nov	Dec
			▨	▨	▨	▨	▨	▨			

Black Garden Ant
Lasius niger

Black Garden Ant

Ants are among the most abundant organisms on Earth. There are 19 ant species in Ireland. Gardens are home to several species of ant, many of which 'farm' aphids for their sweet honeydew. In return, they protect the aphid colonies from attack from natural enemies.

Where to see:

Lasius niger, the Black Garden Ant, is probably the most common ant in Ireland. It is also the ant most often encountered indoors.

Identification:

Black Garden Ants only look black from a distance and are in fact brown. The workers are up to 5mm long.

What they eat:

Ants feed on almost anything but prefer sweet foods. When an ant finds food, it lays a scent to its nest for other workers to follow.

When to see:

Jan	Feb	Mar	Apr	May	Jun	Jul	Aug	Sep	Oct	Nov	Dec

Red Ant
Myrmica rubra

Red Ant

The most commonly found red ant in Irish gardens is *Myrmica rubra*. Most ants don't sting but *Myrmica rubra* is one of the exceptions to this rule. It injects formic acid with its sting which is why it hurts.

Where to see:

It can be found nesting in colonies under stones, in rotting wood and in the soil. *Myrmica rubra* is common and widespread in Ireland and can be found in grasslands and gardens.

Identification:

This ant is approximately 6mm long and is a light reddish colour all over with slightly darker pigmentation on the head.

What they eat:

They are predatory on small insects including aphids.

When to see:

Jan	Feb	Mar	Apr	May	Jun	Jul	Aug	Sep	Oct	Nov	Dec

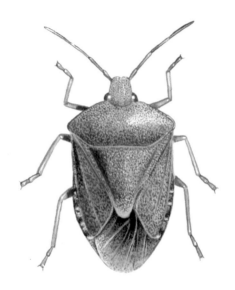

Green Shield Bug
Palomena prasina

Green Shield Bug

The Green Shield Bug is widely found in Ireland and is sometimes called a 'Green Stink Bug' because it produces a pungent odour as a defence mechanism.

Where to see:

It can be seen in gardens on herbaceous plants and shrubs. It can also be seen in parks, on woodland edges and hedgerows.

Identification:

This bug is bright green with tiny black spots in the spring and summer which change to greeny-bronze in the autumn. Its wing tips are dark brown.

What they eat:

Green Shield Bugs suck sap from the leaves of trees, shrubs and herbaceous plants. The nymphs feed on deciduous trees and shrubs, in particular Hazel, *Corylus avellana*.

When to see:

Jan	Feb	Mar	Apr	May	Jun	Jul	Aug	Sep	Oct	Nov	Dec

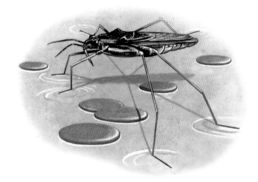

Common Pondskater
Gerris lacustris

Common Pondskater

Pondskaters use their legs to move across the water's surface. They use a rowing action to propel themselves forwards, often at great speed.

Where to see:

These insects are common and widespread in Ireland being found on most stretches of still or slow-moving freshwater habitats.

Identification:

They have thin brownish-grey bodies, very long legs and water-repellent feet. There are several similar-looking species of pondskater in Ireland but as the name suggests, the Common Pondskater, *Gerris lacustris,* is the most widespread.

What they eat:

Pondskaters are predatory and feed on small insects such as midges. Pondskaters catch their prey by sensing vibrations on the water surface of a struggling non-aquatic insect that has fallen into the water.

When to see:

Jan	Feb	Mar	Apr	May	Jun	Jul	Aug	Sep	Oct	Nov	Dec

Common Froghopper
Philaenus spumarius

Common Froghopper

Froghoppers get their name from their ability to jump great distances for their size when under threat.

Where to see:

The Common Froghopper can be seen on woody and herbaceous plants sucking the sap while the larvae can be seen on the plant stems hidden in a small frothy mass. It is a common and widespread species in Ireland.

Identification:

They are small brown insects which can vary greatly in colour. The length of the adult is 5-7mm. Their larvae are commonly seen as a small mass of froth on plant stems. The common name for this is 'cuckoo spit'.

What they eat:

The adults suck plant sap as do most bugs while the larvae eat young leaves.

When to see:

Jan	Feb	Mar	Apr	May	Jun	Jul	Aug	Sep	Oct	Nov	Dec
					■	■	■	■			

Mayfly
(*Ephemeroptera*)

Mayfly

Mayfly are aquatic insects whose immature stage usually last one year in freshwater. The adults are extremely short lived, from a few minutes to a few days depending on the species. There is a total of 33 mayfly species in Ireland.

Where to see:

Mayflies spend most of their life in the water and are extremely important in the diet of fish. They are the models for many of the angler's artificial flies and are therefore often called 'fishing flies'. Adults can be seen dancing above the water on a warm summer day.

Identification:

Stoneflies, caddisflies, and lacewings can sometimes be confused with mayflies but the latter can be identified by their short antennae.

What they eat:

The adults don't feed at all having non-functional mouthparts. Mayfly larvae are herbivorous.

When to see:

Jan	Feb	Mar	Apr	May	Jun	Jul	Aug	Sep	Oct	Nov	Dec

Glossary

Antennae are paired appendages connected to the head of the insect. They are sensory organs.

Cocoon is a pupal casing made by some insect larvae including moths and butterflies.

Elytra are modified hardened forewings of certain insect orders, notably beetles and true bugs.

Larva is the juvenile form of insect and can look completely different from the adult form, for example, a caterpillar looks completely different from a butterfly.

Metamorphosis is the process by which an insect develops involving conspicuous change in animal form.

Pupa is a life stage of some insects undergoing metamorphosis.

Thorax is the division of an insect's body that lies between the head and the abdomen.